SEVEN

MY FIRST TRIP TO THE BANK/
MI PRIMERA VISITA AL BANCO

By Katie Kawa   Traducción al español: Eduardo Alamán

 Gareth Stevens
Publishing

Please visit our website, www.garethstevens.com. For a free color catalog of all our high-quality books, call toll free 1-800-542-2595 or fax 1-877-542-2596.

Library of Congress Cataloging-in-Publication Data

Kawa, Katie.
[My first trip to the bank. Spanish & English]
My first trip to the bank = Mi primera visita al banco / Katie Kawa.
    p. cm. — (My first adventures = Mis primeras aventuras)
In English and Spanish.
Includes index.
ISBN 978-1-4339-6625-5 (library binding)
1. Banks and banking—Juvenile literature. 2. Bank accounts—Juvenile literature. I. Title. II. Title: Mi primera visita al banco.
HG1609.K393 2012
332.1—dc23

                                        2011031669

First Edition

Published in 2012 by
Gareth Stevens Publishing
111 East 14th Street, Suite 349
New York, NY 10003

Copyright © 2012 Gareth Stevens Publishing

Editor: Katie Kawa
Designer: Haley W. Harasymiw
Spanish Translation: Eduardo Alamán

All Illustrations by Planman Technologies

Printed in the United States of America

CPSIA compliance information: Batch #CW12GS: For further information contact Gareth Stevens, New York, New York at 1-800-542-2595.

Contents

- -

Contenido

I have a blue piggy bank.
I keep my money in it.

Tengo una alcancía azul.
Ahí guardo mi dinero.

Today, I am going
to a big bank.

Hoy, voy a un banco.

People keep their money
at the bank.

Las personas guardan
su dinero en el banco.

Banks lend people
money too.

Además, los bancos
le prestan dinero a
las personas.

First, my mom and I
wait in a line.

Primero, mamá y yo
esperamos en la fila.

Then, a worker helps us.
She is called a teller.

Luego, una empleada
nos ayuda. Ella es
una cajera.

I give her my money.

Yo le doy mi dinero.

17

It goes in a safe room.
This is called the vault.

Mi dinero va a una
habitación segura.
A esta habitación se
la llama bóveda.

19

Only bank workers
can go in it.

Sólo los trabajadores
del banco pueden
entrar en la bóveda.

21

My day at the bank
was fun. I hope we
come back soon!

Es divertido ir al banco.
¡Espero regresar muy
pronto!

23

Words to Know/ Palabras que debes saber

piggy bank/
(la) alcancía

teller/
(la) cajera

vault/
(la) bóveda

Index / Índice

24